Some Things That Have Happened So Far

BACKLASH
PRESS

A pioneering publishing house dedicated to creating intelligent, vivid books. Established to inform, educate, entertain and provoke.

A Backlash Press Book

First published 2022
Reprinted 2024

backlashpress.com

Book designer: The Scrutineer, Rachael Adams.

Printed and bound by IngramSpark

ISBN: 978-1-7391016-1-9

All rights reserved. No part of this publication may be reproduced, stored in a retrieval system or transmitted in any form or by any means, electronic, mechanical, photocopying, recording or otherwise, without permission of the copyright holder.

Copyright © G Culshaw
The moral rights of the author have been asserted.

G Culshaw

Some Things That Have Happened So Far G Culshaw

Backlash Poetry

American Dangerous: Renée Olander
Bombing the Thinker: Darren C. Demaree
Burial Machine: Jacob Griffin Hall
Clay Unbreakables: Natalia I Andrievskikh
Into The The: Robin Reagler
Phantom Laundry: Michael Tyrell
Tattered Scrolls and Postulates: Joseph V Milford
The Arsonist's Letters: Michael Tyrell
The Life in the Sky Comes Down: Bruce Bromley
Unfinished Murder Ballads: Darren C. Demaree

Backlash Journals

#1
#2
#3: Provoke
#4
Isolation
#5

Some Things That Have Happened So Far

G Culshaw

Some Things That Have Happened So Far G Culshaw

Dedicated to Matt & Archie for guiding me through life.

Contents

The Day I left School	11
Getting Ready For Winter As A Boy	13
Fishing With Sandwiches	15
Sometimes I Should Have Stayed At Home	17
I Hated Junior School And Everything It Stood For	19
The Grandparent Who Lived Inside Four Walls	21
One Day We Walked To DIY Store	23
Every Year He Brought Out The Roller Tray	25
The Morning Walk To School And Into Teacher's Nostrils	27
Beethoven Lived In My Bedroom	29
Laying Bricks Before Hometime	31
It Was His Shed In The Garden	33
The Neighbour Who Hated Our Football	35
The Watcher	37
Saturday Morning Tennis	39
I Only Knew Him By His Colour	41
I Went Yesterday To See If He Knew I Was There	43
The Last Days Of Childhood I Chased Years Later	45
Weekends When We Were Kids	47
The Tale Of Jarman Avenue	49
Trespassing	51
Mother	53
The Apprentice Of The Backyard	55
The Last Few Years Before She Went Into A Home	57
Before Al Zab His Name Was Adam	59
Lime Street	61
The Long Weekend	63
I Was Half His Size	65
Conwy Castle	67
A Flute Of Wind	69
When I Was A Paperboy I Delivered To An Old Man	71
Timeline	73
Manure	75

Some Things That Have Happened So Far G Culshaw

A Peg Was Taken Out	77
The Bike Ride This Morning	79
One Of Those Teenage Walks I Remember	81
The Third Bedroom	83
He Told Me About Trains	85
An Empty Sack Race	87
Crazy Golf	89
My Parents Lived In A Wood	91
Painting Was All He Did	93
A Train Journey In The Summer Of 1988	95
We Were Young Before We Were Old	97
I Was Once A Spy In Russia	99
His Boots	101
Gas Lamps	103
Taid	105
Yoke	107
The Sea-Front	109
We Went Again Years Later	111
The Matchstick	113
Fire Years	115
Going To Work Empty	117
The First Ten Years Of My Life	119
I Read Them Now	121
The Tail End Of Belongings	123
A Letter To Tom	125
The Follower	133

Some Things That Have Happened So Far G Culshaw

The Day I Left School

The day I left school I found an apple cut in half on the road.
Plumber-tutted as kids squeezed between my coat buttons,
leaving their youth hanging from my ear lobes.
Watched a man remove a pawn line of box hedging, noticed
a window cleaner wipe cobwebs off glass to an empty house.
A taxi went by, nipple pressed its horn, woke up a crow that stood
on top of a lamppost. Seagull's tumble-dryer spun above
a supermarket car park. A salt & vinegar crisp packet tried to hide
behind a fence. I walked the sunlight's back, and felt the heat
leave my soles. My school combed hair became my own.
I joiner-winked at a younger self who skipped a curb.
My crescent fingernails started to grow as a teenage field
terraced my chin. I was already an adult, swearing before I
got home, shoulders strutted like a jaw full of chewing gum.
Our avenue opened as a childhood wound.

I entered the house, hung my coat, dropped a bag, undid
the noose of tie. Two parents sat in the living room
with ornament feet. Garden gnome stared. I glanced
at the grey strands brambling their hair, smoothed their wrinkles
with my tongue. Waited for a conversation of what to do next.

Some Things That Have Happened So Far G Culshaw

Getting Ready for Winter as a Boy

I watched him bring out sellotape as his hands shook
with January. We taped keyholes, unrolled a draught excluder
for the windows cut strips for their plastic frames to shut
away the frosty words. He bought a new rug, lowered it down
as a first aider with an injured body. I stood, noticing the stars
flicker as if living off a gas hob. A curtain hung above
the front door. He changed his newspaper eyes to a DIY setting.
A pulled blind became a tube of tin foil for a turkey dinner.
Summer coat retired, a thicker one walked out of an Index Catalogue.
Chatter of a Siberian frost, or Polar winds, threatened to leave us
dead in bed for weeks until a neighbour noticed our empty bin.
A loaf of snow waited in the sky ready to cavity the gaps in hedges,
or keep the oldies indoors as they wrinkled like out-of-date sprouts.
My socks thickened with each wash. I lost my feet. A hat slowed
my growth. He brought out curtains with extra backing.
Swapped summer quilts for fresh bread thickness. I cocooned,
unaware the outside was still alive.

Some Things That Have Happened So Far G Culshaw

Fishing with Sandwiches

In biscuit summers we fished. Took our mouths to a river
that belted up earth from tarmac. Our voices drank sunlight.
Tree canopies thumbled clouds across a leaf sky.
A shade fell out of a crisp packet. We set up rods, fixed weights,
watched wriggling maggots bend into alphabet letters.

Liquid leather brushed over cysts of rock, punctured fish roads.
Once ready, we flipped back hope, flung school homework
into the skies mirror. A sandwich crept out of a bag, clamped
by fingers too small to break pencils.

A Casio watch told us when parents arrived home from work.
Fish, teased us with slipper slaps on the edges, or a plop of air
from gills. They winked at us when we closed our eyes
from a sun that beamed off the cling film. A tub of maggots
threatened to explode if touched.

Bringing back the rod, hooks, javelin-stabbed a Science-lesson thumb.
Leaves grew over our heads, nudging away T-shirt sunlight. Coldness
shuffled jumpers. We sighed. One or two caught a minnow. Chocolate
filled the mouth's gutter. Burps crowed as fizzy pop turned flat
bellies into gas cylinders.

We sat until crackers came out, then packed up for the haul home.
Water, lemon-squeezed out of our trainers. Streetlights panicked us
down adult roads. On the street, we atom-split, entered our parents'
mouths with wet socks, broken tans, and the smell of sawdust
that kept maggots dry. A page turn of night, we went to school,
behaved as if none of us knew each other.

Some Things That Have Happened So Far G Culshaw

Sometimes I Should have Stayed at Home

A road bled cars as I lumbered to his clock-ticking house.
He would be folding his morning into dinnertime. Youth hung
off my face though I never felt it drip to the floor. Months after
leaving school this road became a tunnel to an adult.

Take-Two video store closed down, Marion's Newspaper shop
clouded my eyesight. The Costume Place gave its customers
to the Internet. Jones the Butcher's hooked itself to people's lives.
The flies sensed rotting meat as they lingered outside with spliffs
and beer. A local chippy fell to the Turks who cut kebab
joints in the window. A cucumber grin hid within stubble.

I knew he was in, as the gate was locked, and the kitchen shivered
from a fluorescent light. Garden cobwebs draped fly bodies and dust,
spiders waited with paperboy legs for the next round. I saw him,
pottering, with words in his mouth ready to drop off moss-eyebrows.

I knocked, entered with grape-crushing feet, caught a frown
in his bread crust. He glanced, salted a tomato, tilted a pot of tea.
The dog sat under the table covered in the years she's known.
I cut my body in half and dropped onto the wooden chair.
Heard the knife in the butter tub. We exchanged words for silence,
gave the clock its tick, sighed away a day I tend to forget.

Some Things That Have Happened So Far G Culshaw

I Hated Junior School and Everything it Stood For

Junior school plagued my childhood as a hornet stuck in my head.
Black P.E pumps, protractors for maths, calculators to find home.
Plastic butty box with sandwiches placed inside bread bags.
Hair, parted to one side, made me lose balance as I walked.

Grey trousers brought teachers to my life. Their eyes fed
my brain wormed their way along channels filling my head
full of characters my life was too slow to know.
My fingernails tapped dusty books as spider legs on a saucer.

The world, flat back then, allowed sunlight to run away
form puddles for my journey home. P.E lessons hung ropes
off the sky. A horse box waited to throw me from my mother.

The Head Teacher grew with trees walked with hobnobs in a pocket,
and a cup of tea, balancing on his tongue. We never saw his eyes,
aware a fire lingered from his first bonfire night. I would play
football, or sit somewhere, where woodlice listened to the winds.

Some Things That Have Happened So Far G Culshaw

The Grandparent Who Lived Inside Four Walls

The four dogs he owned during his life were stuffed on the landing.
Their eyes followed as you library-coughed to the upstairs loo.
Sunlight squeezed through a door window as a letter in an envelope.
Stair treads winced with each step, nudged the after-rain-silence.
Photos hung on woodchip wallpaper as portholes in a ship.
Ceiling cracks became palm prints where he'd pushed back the sky.
The hallway, a gap in his teeth, and you heard the echo in his voice.
A hazel walking stick helped him visit the outside or a flat cap
kept a summer sun off his frail hair line. He lintel-frowned.
Ate cake with a dog jaw and swallowed his morning before dinner.

The next-door neighbour walked by with a promenade cadence
turned to the window as if he'd seen bird shit on the glass.
I sat with a folded newspaper, heard the call of a wood pigeon.
He fell asleep with a sleeping bag restless. I felt my life fall
from my fingers as rain off leaves. I returned two weeks later
heard a pigeon coo.

Some Things That Have Happened So Far G Culshaw

One Day We Walked To A DIY Store

Through the garden gate along a cracked sky,
you hobbled, I walked. Gap of years between us
sang in the song of a local blackbird. Your silver hair
polished sunlight rays as my own scruffy top
went with the day's wind. We angled ourselves
until a flat tarmac pavement led us to street signs,
open roads. Dog oil and Brylcreem flicked off
your tongue as you gasped words between medicated lips.

You tapped at things with your stick, prodded yesterday,
checked the edge of your eyebrows. Your frown, lay
as a dog by a back door. I kept my legs from gathering
pace tutted with wings of a startled pigeon, then sighed,
knowing your clock ticked with each step.

In this here and now episode, a freshness came over me
like the start of a new day through an open letterbox.
Only years later did I realise such a thing as I walked
my own pavement with a hint of hip pain.

Some Things That Have Happened So Far G Culshaw

Every Year He Brought Out The Roller Tray

Every year a room was painted with horse hair brushes.
Lampshades taken off as helmets on tired cyclists. Later on,
a living room light filled the room as if the sun had been lowered.
The odd petal of paint stubbed on a sofa arm or book shelf.
Fumes filled my nostrils as foam in a cavity wall. He told us about
the difference between matt and silk. How woodchip wallpaper
was being replaced by embossed. His voice slipped with the strokes
of his brush as blue jeans held previous paint jobs.
Stoic walls glimmered like ice on a mountain. I saw snowballs
in the thicker dabs. Half a tin sat outside, squatted under the stars,
brushes stood in a tub of turps.

A roller tray lay upside down as hot water dripped after cleaning.
The lampshade sat on the kitchen table. Rolls of wallpaper hung
around in a living room corner. Once the paint became the outer
skin of an onion, a fresh carpet was laid. White walls reached up
into the ceiling, the room became an igloo.
We sat inside his colour for years, except the floor, where a new
pattern made us take our slippers off, allowing our feet to breathe.

Some Things That Have Happened So Far G Culshaw

The Morning Walk To School And Into Teacher's Nostrils

Walking to school through the fly of the adult world
was something we enjoyed more than school dinnertime.
Seeing people in work clothes, chewing coffee,
slurping a hot bacon roll, or zig zagging away a hangover.
These were mornings we didn't understand, but picked
out what we thought we needed for later years.
High viz men, faces from oil paintings, stonewall knuckles
carried cigarettes and flasks of home.

The odd suit ironed their way up the road, a black tie hung
off a neck too thin to use at a footy match. Garden-flower
mother's anchored little kids to purse hands, spoke to them
with crow voices above a ploughed field.

Sometimes there were three of us, maybe four, or even two.
In winter, gloves and hoods scratched us away from people's
memories. In summer, we strutted with gelled hair,
white fingernails, and a waft of Lynx. I remember seeing
an older version of myself in the walking stick of a man.

He wore a flat cap, brown belt and carried a shopping bag
full of rain. I saw him again this morning, coming over
the hill of my chin, as I shaved.

Some Things That Have Happened So Far G Culshaw

Beethoven Loved In My Bedroom

When I was a boy, I opened the curtains heard Beethoven
in the mouth of a blackbird. My football shorts folded
themselves in drawers I knew school clothes hid inside.
Leaves fell off a council hedge as father trimmed away
another summer banquet where tennis balls and trainers
bounced around a tarmac floor. I sat on a bed waited
for the violin to calm down dreams that plagued my brain.
Sunlight painted over shadows. Dust hovered in my room
like midges over cow pats. The cassette reached the end,
silence fed itself out of speakers bought from Asda.
I stood up, entered the cloud, walked downstairs
to television and newspapers. Found mother collapsed
in her own weight, heard father taking away memories
we had grown.

So, I sat, wondering if Beethoven was still alive.

Some Things That Have Happened So Far G Culshaw

Laying Bricks Before Hometime

I used to lay bricks on the brow of a cloud.
Heard rain fall into my ear canal to flood my brain.
The trowel tapped the silence I brought from home.
Music fizzed through a radio as we mixed sand and water
slapped baguette shaped mortar onto a wall that grew
with lunch breaks. Fingernails full of greyness coloured
my hair. When I showered, I rubbed away youth found
before stubble scoured my face. A cement mixer turned
itself around as birds watched with eyes like struck matches.
Rain fell through the wear and tear of summer, a shovel
leaned itself against a rusty van, bricks lay on pallets
waiting for their purpose in life.

Sunlight wept out of the mouth of my boss as he lit
another fag. His teeth worn with the old stone wall
we were replacing. I carried bricks, felt the weight of the job.
Caught a sparrow flying through two holes in jeans
mother bought me. We built the wall with an English Bond
turned quiet bricks into sun-stained foreheads. Watched a dog
piss against three gate posts. Heard cats scrap for the silence
of a garden hammock. Perps haemorrhage mortar as I laid
each brick like I was back in childhood with Lego.
Sweat, paint-dripped down my forehead, dust coughed itself
out of a throat I found in the first pub I drank in.
My boss rested against sun rays propped himself up
on two spades. He whistled with a keyhole mouth.
I looked at my trowel, found the handle too thick to hold,
felt a cloud rest on shoulders that slumped homeward.

Some Things That Have Happened So Far G Culshaw

It Was His Shed In The Garden

We had a shed that sat in the tamed back garden
a wooden igloo with spider webs cutting away the corners.
Every summer holiday he painted our eyes with creosote.
Used block brushes to wipe away splinters, and last winter.
A set of draws filed records and books. Himself.
Garden tools hung their weight off nails, tapped
in the breeze when the door was open. A lawnmower stayed
quiet. He kept toilet rolls, bleach, cleaning wipes, tissues,
bin bags and anything else the house couldn't handle.
A shelf ran along the wall with screws and washers,
the odd battery, sellotape, hair. As a child I never went inside.
Looked at the roof from my bedroom window found the felt
to be a mirror of the night sky with its hint of sand.

When I got older, I started to enter this shell of darkness noticed
holes in the panels as the sun shot tubes of light.
I think it's where he used to go if the house became too much.

Some Things That Have Happened So Far G Culshaw

The Neighbour Who Hated Football

I saw him watching as his eyes flamed from behind glass.
His hair fed itself into the curtains, but we saw his shadow
fall onto his lawn, lit up by his ceiling light.

The tongue he lived with lay in his mouth, waiting for the ball
to enter his garden, then it unleashed itself with a lizard-lick
of the air we breathed. He grabbed the weekend under his arm,
used a swear word that stung the ears we grew.

The tan he found one summer as a child was replaced by
the cholesterol of work. His forehead showed wrinkles
as wheel tracks in mud. We laughed at his speed of feet,
but ran away, in case his hands caught our throats and broke
the denim off our legs.

He threw the ball back with the release of air, like a tin
opener on a can of tuna. His wife, divorced from life lived
somewhere in the house ran through his veins when he shouted
from his garden shed. As I aged, I found out who he was.
An older version of myself.

Some Things That Have Happened So Far G Culshaw

The Watcher

He wasn't someone I knew though his name hung outside
his house. His red door stood against blue moonlight.
We walked by, aware of him watching from behind the window.
Our footballs lay under kitchen tables, but he still kept an eye
on our heads like a summer sun on a puddle.

We winked our feet sipped cans of Vimto until the stomach bowed,
and threw a grenade burp into our mouths. We both watched him.
Laughed at his egg-shell belly, and the wellies he wore going for chips.
His lips letterboxed his mouth. Telephone wires tent polled the sky.
A sparrow scratched the blackness as a match on sandpaper.

We sat on the steps heard clouds shimmy across our foreheads
as slippers on carpet. He stood watching. His eyes turned his house
into a head. A car pulled up the road tugged its owner home after work.
Stars pickled themselves as a waft of cigarette smoke whispered
across our minds. We looked up, and he was stood by the hedge,
wondering why we were out in the dark.

Some Things That Have Happened So Far G Culshaw

Saturday Morning Tennis

We filled a tennis court with the dirty laundry of teenage years.
Swore with gull tongues, laughed at crayon-haired joggers.
Whacked the hell out of a cyst that school had swapped
with our brains. Spat onto a brush that swept up autumn.
A dog walker watched with two blinks of mascara before
carrying on with last night's wine.

The ball bounced as if trying to jump the fence to find a dog's mouth.
Orange cordial lit the corner. Three kids ran through a gate
lost in the maze of childhood. We both shook our heads
to rid memories of what we knew and they didn't.

A crow, pecked leaf mould, found a point I lost three games ago.
A council worker followed the park's path. Built plaque
on his teeth from cola bubbles as he swigged with his left hand.
Sunlight gave us the glow of Tesco at night. A chimney popped
smoke that looked like a white sky between tree canopies.

Clouds became thrown bread. We played until frowns weighed
down smiles we brought in wallets. Scone foreheaded, I gasped
for a chicken lung of air, as he swung his racket to hit another ball.
My elbow bent as the branch of an apple tree when scrumping.
We both lost that Saturday morning, but neither remember why.
I wait for you to tell me.

Some Things That Have Happened So Far G Culshaw

I Only Knew Him By His Colour

I only knew him as blackbird. He came each morning
before the toast was buttered. Though he never knocked,
he was always inside our house before we got up.

I caught him in the rain balancing on a raindrop.
His feathers scorched by too much sun as a child
he hopped around as if his feet were still hot.

When the wind came he stayed in the hedge
saddled his song on a twig. In snow, he stood out
as a black sheep. We knew he was a good guy,

and let him carry on picking worms, woodlice,
and ants. I never knew his name, only blackbird.
His beak had been dipped into the sun each morning.

His song fell from a place we did not know, but had been
told about in books. I wondered if it's where he lived,
when we closed our eyes, and the world turned black.

Some Things That Have Happened So Far G Culshaw

I Went Yesterday To see If He Knew I Was There

I went yesterday. Walked in the morning light,
a sunray through a bottle of olive oil.
A moult of clouds filled in the gaps of lost words.
I turned the corner like I was a tin opener.
Caught a sky I played footie under as a boy.
Wondered if the flakes of leather still lingered
in fence panels of people who hated our way.
The road, a fabric of material in my brain.
I tried to stitch up street signs as I walked.
The old folk we've lost, glimmering in the slug
trails of lost gardens. House doors grinned as I passed,
neighbours poked my face as they heard me whistling
up the wheelie bin road. Recycling tubs tab-keyed.
A blob of a car sat at the top. Hedges reformed
their shape now we'd moved out. I knew he was in.
Curtains half-closed like a sleeping butterfly.
The ceiling light, kestrel hovered, above the room.
Door unlocked, I entered the shell of childhood.
He sat as a fisherman on the edge of a pond.
I entered his head. Three hours later, I left.

Some Things That Have Happened So Far G Culshaw

The Last Days of Childhood I Chased Years later

These were the last days of childhood as my feet stamped stud marks into a council field. An odd adult watched from a sideline brought an alleyway-whistle. I knew you were standing inside your mouth. White lines fed themselves into clouds moulded a pitch that surrounded my mind. I ran past people, kicked a ball, unaware these were the minutes falling from my eyelids at night. I saw the length of childhood as we ran after empty spaces.

Parents brought work clothes or shopping lists, talked about bills at half-time. We ran around each other swarmed with daydream innocence. Boot-shaped lungs gasped for words. Syrup-sweat fell from open forehead wounds. Fingernails, clean of work, calcium shone in the moonlight's wake. The scoreline tick tocked in our heads as I walked off.

I felt the result of these years when I became lost in a January wood. Walking through branch-shaped sunlight hearing the call of a newspaper wind. I carried on until I forgot who I had been, but found them in leaves that crunched underfoot.

Some Things That Have Happened So Far G Culshaw

Weekends When We were Kinds

As the sun broke up the night I opened as a dandelion.
My feet stretched under the duvet, dreams fell out of my ears.
Curtains gasped as I pulled them apart as light fed into my
eye-crust. One or two heads would be kicking the ball
with sleepy feet. Sparrows, market stalls jabbered. A quick
wash and I was released from my parents. The odd cloud
smudged open our future as words chased away bat trails.
A neighbour's cat licked mouse blood or Felix off its paws.
Other lads gathered until our tide was ready to swamp summer.
An adult took their car from one of the garages, pulled it out
as a cigar from a mouth.

Someone held the ball with a teapot arm. We kicked off
blinking with butterfly wing eyelids. School, the day
after tomorrow, as we played to win the FA Cup.
This the era of embossed wallpaper, a sky dish, double-glazing,
electric lawnmowers, folding doors bought from DO-IT-ALL.
Older people hung on with hedge shears and hoover bags.
None of us thought these days slipped by with each school lesson.
Even parents started to grow away from our childhood.
We kicked until patches peeled and paint fell off garage doors.
We tried to keep up the sun, before succumbing to itchy stars,
and homework, that simmered in sporty bags.

Some Things That Have Happened So Far G Culshaw

The Tale Of Jarman Avenue

When the swifts came to the terraced eves
and brought their flight above our youth
we played under sun's swollen heat
brushed our fingers against avenue leaves.
Throats spat out phlegm on the crow-pecked road.
We kicked a ball for the sound of rubber
poured music into our embossed ears.

Below our bony feet the world turned seasons,
but at night, bat wings grew from our eyelids.
We walked in showers, ran down hours, slept at home.
Picked at tar that sellotaped pavements
crushed ants with our tree-ringed fingerprints.
Behaved as if the adult world was known.
Wore shorts to buy ice-cream, licked them clean
like dogs on bone.

Someone's gran passed away and we sat in silence.
Heard her voice in the letterbox wind.
None of us knew that life came after this,
or this street had another street at the bend.
Shoulders nudged a strut. Our tongues fell to stutter
when the girls came out with field-wind hair,
and our asparagus fingers yet to touch
the pink skin that wrapped their salt-white bone.

When school left me I was up in the loft
looking through the skylight of my eyes.
Searched for the butter coloured path I dreamt
that sniggered between these fag-ash homes.
Over time friendships became a disturbed flock
lost in the hours of tick-tock. Old footprints faded
into the ground, between garden fences

Some Things That Have Happened So Far G Culshaw

there was no sound.

The holiday scars from teenage days
now bandaged by wounds of adult years.
I never grasped what we had that summer.
Though now I know that darkness lingers deep
and the clavicle pergolas the minutes worked.

Today I lean on the bar that brows the quay
hear the gulls above with cracker-laughter.
I think of home and the avenue I have known
as I watch my life wash away on the beaches rind.
When I was young, I watched a sky fall low
and it helped the swifts to come and go.

Long-listed in the Yaffle Poetry Competition 2020

Trespassing

When I walk into the wood before morning
catch a flick of blackbird out of the holly
sniff the tail of a fox on his last round,
watch the sun lower the moon, I wait for him.

I meander through his sleep, even the leaves
below my feet, don't stir. There's fog
swirling as smoke in a glass bottle.
I listen to the silence of his breath.

The hedgerows start to flame with spring.
A woodpecker begins to wake
up the trees. I am cloud-light, aware
of my trespassing.

My eyes allow more light into my brain
as I watch a bee bring its shape to the wood.
The night peels itself off the sky. I try
to catch him before the world turns east.

My hearing grasps at the earth. A sock
of mole brings up soil, a hand-grenade
of robin drops its pin, but the morning stays
deep. And with it, allows me to find who

I am in the emptiness of God.

Winner of the RS Thomas Competition Eglwys Fach 2019

Some Things That Have Happened So Far G Culshaw

Mother

Mother sat in the chair her body
a boulder I saw in Snowdonia.
He hair had become limestone grey
the youthful black lost to the winds.
Her eyes kept her face alive showed me
two conkers I once found in a wood.
I sat behind a newspaper waited
for him to leave the room. When he did,
the walls exhaled as if the house
had taken a deep breath.
I knew Mother's days had been cured
by his words as salt on meat.
When I was a child she had a voice
that crashed against the sky as waves on
sea walls. I preferred it when she was on mute
lost in the tick of the clock.
I folded up the newspaper and we spoke,
two owls, calling across a field,
the distance growing with each birthday.
I never felt we would leave each other
to walk the streets alone, but when I left
home, I listened each night for her reply.

Some Things That Have Happened So Far G Culshaw

The Apprentice in The Backyard

He chewed the sunlight as if it was tobacco.
The saw fissured wood until the board sounded
like three dropped golf balls on a floorboard.

He straightened his spine, cracked away winter.
Cobwebs fell from his armpits. He was back working
again, but this time on the mind of his teenage grandson.

He bent down used the shark teeth to mow
away the pencil line he had drawn. His arm pistoned
the morning light, pulled up the daytime.

He passed me the tenon saw. It hung from my hand
as a carcass. He watched from the side as the sun
does when lighting the moon.

I edged ahead put my thumb by the line, dragged
the saw until I heard the morning break.
After a few seconds my hand had moved off the line.

I felt his fox eyes behind my head, heard his breathe
as if I was being hunted. He lowered himself.
His hands, the colour of decking stain, shuffled towards mine.

Spirit-level eyes, sliding-bevel arm, set-square head,
he stabilized my youth, brought the saw back to the mark.
Showed me the direction I'd been searching since birth.

Some Things That Have Happened So Far G Culshaw

The Last Few Years Before She Went Into A Home

Her legs are fag ends in an ashtray
stubbed out by his mouth.
She hasn't walked since the solar panels
went up. Tells me the sun is inside
the house so there's no point going out.
Curtains half-closed, television - a gap
in the clouds, and she sits searching
for the next life. He presses the remote buttons
changes the volume with his pork tongue.
Her pill-box is a mechanics socket set.
She drops one every hour, tilts her head
like a bird drinking from a puddle of rain.
They both sit there as tent pegs hammered
into the ground by the weight of the sky.
When bedtime comes the stairs carry
her to the top, and he follows with seagull
wings after a fishing trawler.

Some Things That Have Happened So Far G Culshaw

Before Al Zab His Name Was Adam

He wears shoes that are a size too small.
Struggles to carry shopping home
because of his hernia.

His wife left him years ago, ran off with a postie.
They now deliver letters. She does the odd
numbers and he does the even.

He talks about the seventies like it's the nineties
until his neighbour closes the windows on him.
Then he walks up and down the sky

whistles folk songs that play in his head.
He stretches his washing across two lines.
The garden becomes a tent three days a week.

From behind, his neck seems to be giving birth
to an egg. His moustache, nicked from a cloud,
that he once walked under drunk.

He has war medals on a plasterboard wall. Shivers
nightmares at three am. Rumour has it he was lost
in Al Zab for two days.

To survive, he ate the fingers of a dead soldier.
When the back-up team arrived they saw him curled
up like a dog behind a hedge.

On the drive out of there he picked out
a fingernail from between his teeth. Told his officer
he'd left his name behind.

Some Things That Have Happened So Far G Culshaw

Lime Street

Plastic chairs moulded into the wall.
Our voices became lost in the tunnel,
and blackness tubed each side of the platform.

I felt I was inside a brain with all the nattering
and prattle. Mother sat, allowed her day
to rest. Father walked about, newspaper rolled

under his arm like a map. People gathered,
inched their way to the white line as cattle
to a freshly filled trough.

Their voices louder than at the station back home
they seemed to have more words to use
tongues slapped the silence as a whale's tail on water.

The rails screeched as two eyes lit up on the bend.
Doors pulled themselves apart, feet jumped
off, others stepped on, luggage wheels mowed the dust.

We waited for our train, mother sat in the moulded seat,
father looked at the time, and I, caught in-between.

Some Things That Have Happened So Far G Culshaw

The Long Weekend

Stew bubbled in the kitchen; father grabbed the teapot
and filled it with boiling water. Joe hunched in his chair
as a barrel of homebrew sat stubbornly on the shelf.
The tap, a gateway to someplace else. His white
hair thinned by filtered pints. Gran scuffed her way
from room to room. Me and mum took the settee
while chatter mixed with the television.
Everything slowed down in here after the burst
of a walk from the bus stop. Now father sat on a creaky
chair and filled cups of tea as gran ladled the kitchen.
Horse racing on the television sped things up again,
their tongues jumped each other's words,
hooves stamped down mine and mother's thoughts.
Gran brought in the bowls, gave us bread slapped in butter.
We hamster nibbled, dog slurped, and our working class
tongue felt heat from the moments of silence.

Some Things That Have Happened So Far G Culshaw

I Was Half His Size

Those days in the cemetery walking along the paths
that were being forced up by the roots of trees.

Marble gravestones inched their way to the floor
became drawbridges for sunlight.

The tap that dripped when tight, gushed when open.
Pots of flowers filled, then brought back to her date.

I was half the height of you back then. Wondered what
the other half would bring. There was silence and a vast

sky above. Her chiselled name stung the marble. I never
treaded on her lawn thinking maybe one day she would

come back. But all the time you stood there knowing
that the other half of my growth was the slowest lived.

And felt the same day, after day, after day.

Some Things That Have Happened So Far G Culshaw

Conwy Castle

The stones held each other above the town.
Arrow slits in the walls told me the sea
was out there being dragged back by the moon.

The turrets allowed steps to twist inside them.
My whole foot was able to step on each rise.
Father followed as the sun anchored his lungs.

I put my head between the merlons, peered
through the embrasure, and looked at rooftops,
roads, people, gulls and a world I did not see

when down there. Father reached the top,
and his breathing pulled me away.
As he looked, he saw the sky, and told me

Ireland lay at the end of his finger. My eyes
widened to another country's name. He said
about other places, mapped the earth for me

before I went to secondary school. After we
got home I heard him tell mum the rooms
of the house and where things went.

But I hadn't realised she already knew.

Some Things That Have Happened So Far G Culshaw

A Flute of Wind

Outside there is a flute wind.
The Nursing Home is a wood of fallen trees.
I see a woman with cow parsley hair
lying in bed as I make my way through
the marribone corridors.
My feet, like pianist hands,
tune-in the floorboards with every step.
Her room is as small as the earth
with closed eyes.
I enter the memories we shared.
Mother's legs are fettered by arthritis
as they lie on a bull-neck bed.
She is now in the metamorphoses,
and the tears fall from me at night
as I sleep.

Some Things That Have Happened So Far G Culshaw

When I was A Paperboy I Delivered To An Old Man

Eggshells are placed all over the carpet. Dust rubs onto your
clothes as you enter the hallway. A pair of boots stand within
themselves, four pairs of slippers lie like beaver tails, one flip flop
held last summer. He walks towards us, holding a pair of glasses
on his nose. A whisper comes out of his mouth as a draught.
I try to hear, turn my head, catch the words that have slipped
off his photo album face. Council worker bones rummage under
clothes as if he's shedding skin. Wardrobe coldness hangs
in the air. As he walks to the front door his legs are brushes
in a road sweeper's hands. He picks out a bag of coins from
his pocket. The left hand rollercoaster shakes. I see the eyes
are starting to peel old age under chipboard eyelids. He passes
me coins. I count them with my school trained brain give him
today's newspapers. He reads the headlines, forces a grin.
I turn to leave the hallway, open the sky, and see the sun hang
above a rooftop like a kite. He locks the door before I open the gate.

Some Things That Have Happened So Far G Culshaw

Timeline

It's my time now to pick up,
wipe clean, mop yesterday.
Opening out, locking in,
bring the sun to the door

as and when. They sit
watching photo albums
fall from their minds. Voices
been and gone, their lives

fall back down their throat
into a pit of darkness that I
try to steer them away from.
It's my time now to pick up

the dead skin that has built
and hides in the corners of settees
thickened on window sills
greyed the in-between on remote

control buttons clouded the light
bulbs that hang and sit.
It's up to me now to pick up
the timeline they have seeded,

as I ready myself to walk alone,
until the next time.

Some Things That Have Happened So Far G Culshaw

Manure

We went when the world was as big as a Monday morning.
Our bodies gave the sun - light, as we walked up the road.

The wheelbarrow turned its wheel, laid out the path as it thumbled.
I was garden gate-high, and noticed houses prop up the perspex sky.

We entered the allotments as voices in a tunnel. Father picked up
a rusty fork filled the barrow with clumps of manure.

His back heaved up clouds, knees wobbled from carrying
a weight he did not experience in his own job.

When we got home he tipped it onto his potatoes. The smell
told me about summer months and why farmers wear flat-caps.

The spuds would grow as big as lie-ins he said, taste like Christmas,
and we would be digging them up until I left school.

Weeks later, nothing changed, and we wondered if the path
had been the right one.

Some Things That Have Happened So Far G Culshaw

A Peg Was taken Out

The house was sandwiched into a terraced row.
Slates angled the sunlight, chimneys were heads
through jumpers. Phone wires tied us all together
to save our dreams floating away.
There were four of us, two in the front, two
in the back. Voices ranged in height. We had names,
talked to each other through different teeth.
When Christmas came presents were bricks
left behind at a building site. A tree filled the corner,
decorations spread across the white painted walls.
One day I came downstairs to see kitchen paper
on the floor. A doctor closed up his bag to keep
away the night, walked out in vicar shoes.
Weeks later, there were two adults in the front,
one child in the back, and the house moved in the wind
as a tent with a missing peg.

Some Things That Have Happened So Far G Culshaw

The Bike Ride This Morning

The crow tarmac sizzles.
My tyres turn the wheels
as I ride into a herons mouth
of sunlight.

A car pulls out of a drive
crushes the silence I am in.
I turn up the lane and feel
puddle-moulds under my feet.

Cherry blossom finger-nails
the floor. I keep left until I
turn right. Then I am uphill
and passed the trees.

I lean my bike against a gate
take out binoculars and see
herring fog rise out of the grass.
The sky shapes the sun.

There's light frothing in my eyes
the morning shunts across the land.
The day will start soon, but for a time,
I want this gate to myself,

open it when I feel ready.

Some Things That Have Happened So Far G Culshaw

One Of Those Teenage Walks I Remember

I never saw the end of the road as I cement-mixer-rumbled along the pavement. The sky, a lid. Lamp posts marked distance. Cars beaded as a roundabout pinned down the world.

Rooftops toblerone as I carried on. A bus stop held a tail of people. Two dog walkers broke up the tarmac as I headed for the backroads of farms and country lanes where trees could be themselves, hedgerows moustached fields, and sunlight spread across the skylarks song.

These were the days of loss. Clock batteries ran themselves down as I waited for life to happen. Cambers showed more than school ever had. The odd tractor wheeled by, white vans scrolled a road, farm yards gave me stillness to stare. An odd dog barked from behind a cloud.

Some Things That Have Happened So Far G Culshaw

The Third Bedroom

I know you both suffered when the third bedroom
was not filled and a single bed never grew.

The four walls were kept in the cold.
I was next door, listening.

But her voice never came. The door locked
by a hook and eye loop, curtains half opened.

When you went in there you could have been in her
skull looking at what might have been.

But I knew she was around. I saw her in mother's eyes.

Some Things That Have Happened So Far G Culshaw

He Told Me About Trains

Even now they still fly past like they're laying
down the rails as they go. He told me about trains
how he worked on them between the hours of sun.

The smell of oil stayed in his fingertips. The palms
stained with scrubbing away the working years.
He lit cigarettes in the cabin to warm his hands.

He tapped the platform with hobnailed boots.
After work, he walked five miles to see Hetty,
and laid down the road that sat between them.

He put the stations of his life in my mind.
And when I need to stop someplace, it's always
those platforms I wait at.

Some Things That Have Happened So Far G Culshaw

An Empty Sack Race

The lanes painted by council workers
empty seats lined up one side of the track.
Teachers organised, walked, talked, took notes,
placed infinite pens into hidden pockets.
Parents turned up between adult hours; then chairs
became chairs. I was given a sack to race with,
and at the whistle was told to leap like a frog.
I was never the fastest, or most agile, the fact

my legs disappeared, and feet could not be spoken
to, making reaching the end that bit harder.
Parents clapped as children cheered and screamed.
Their voices gushed into my body, turned my legs
to concrete. I leapt until my legs departed,
and were left in the hessian sack. But what made
things heavier was when I looked to the side,
my parents were not even there.

Some Things That Have Happened So Far G Culshaw

Crazy Golf

It was the one thing I looked forward to,
the putting of a ball that bounced,
bobbed, trickled, or popped off concrete.

A windmill shed, arch, white bunkers,
a wooden see-saw were all various challenges
we had to face on the course.

At first, I never understood how hard to hit,
until I saw you tap away, letting the ball
do the work.

We were one back then, side by side,
as mother sat on the wall listening
to the waves.

I learnt from you, listened to your wise words.
I tried to save the runs of each ball you hit,
in hope they would guide me years later.

We went through the holes. A birdie here
birdie there, the odd bogey. Found routes
to be quick on some, slow on others.

Tapped the ball, heard it roll under the sky,
as doughnut smells filled our eyes.
When I went back years later I saw the winds

had brushed away the paint, rust set in on
the fence, moss gathered on the wall where mother sat.
So, I carried on walking the path you showed me
with a tap of a new golf ball.

Some Things That Have Happened So Far G Culshaw

My Parents Lived In A Wood

The height of summer in a wood
is only noise.

The rain silks the leaves. Umbellifers
try to hold up the sky's floor.

Hoverflies swap positions
like they're manning my memories.

Fledgelings nail their tones
to trees. Outside, the fields are bronze.

I am in the middle of the turn back
to the end of summer.

I see their faces turn to crinkled
leaves. I listen to their diluted words.

Their shadows start to linger.
I want the leaves to go so they have
some light.

But they are migrating, leaving me
alone in this wooden living room.

Some Things That Have Happened So Far G Culshaw

Painting Was All He Did

'Gas and Electric I don't touch'
he once said to me as I tried to catch
his height. But give him a paintbrush,

and he was away with the strokes.
Biting his bottom lip as he cut in,
keeping the colours safe, he placed

the same wall in every room.
He wore light blue jeans that wore
scars of previous paint jobs.

I saw his hair go lighter with each
year after the dust was blown away
for decorating. He never touched

things that connected. The strokes were
all his own, taking them up and down
by himself. We never saw another

house while we lived there. And things
dragged on with each bristle, each stroke.

Some Things That Have Happened So Far G Culshaw

A Train Journey In The Summer Of 1988

Bickering sunlight ran alongside the windows trying to get in.
Teacher shadows grew under my feet as I sat in a football top.
Triangle sandwiches filled my mouth as a foot in a school shoe.
My parents sat in tandem, their eyes lost to misshapen clouds.
Stations went by with names I could not spell. People got on
or off, brought perfume, and sand between their toes.
Chatter exploded if families knew each other, words became
sparklers. A baby screamed like a male fox on a January night.
I remember sitting there unaware of our stop as doughnut
smells and nicotine cirrus clouds took away the air.
With each stop my trouser belt seemed to tighten by another
hole. Chairs became extinct, kids ran up and down as if lost.
I nibbled crisps, counted the bites, and crunched away time.
Mother looked at me, our eyes clashed as rolling pebbles.
The sun ran alongside the train. I watched clouds bunker
the sky and the rays of light got jammed within each other.
Shadows grew. My trouser belt tightened. The air being sucked
up by adults whose lungs were much bigger than mine.
I vacuumed what I could, took a swig of Panda Cola,
looked at my father, his eyes closed up as shop shutters.
The train went on for miles, as I sat, unaware of our stop.

Some Things That Have Happened So Far G Culshaw

We Were Young Before We Became Old

When young we looked up at the stars
to see if they would ever stop shaking.
The fizz of youth held in the palm
of our hands. In school we put it in the back
pocket of Asda bought trousers.
Adults held moustaches, grew sideburns,
smoked lung busters, drank whiskey, and wore
ties to hold back petal words in their throat,
Neighbours aged quicker than us. Wrinkles
scuffed up their faces, lichen-eyebrows hid
eyes we had yet to see. Some putted the day
with walking sticks, others sighed, as they staggered
up the street with carrier bags.
One or two mowed bumpy lawns, or painted fences
with creosote. Hedgetrimmers came out of sheds,
cut away birdsong. Garden gates had a year of four
seasons brushed off their frames.
An old man whistled with a lollipop shaped mouth
his hair stuffed in his top pocket, carried a penknife
to undo the clouds that hung like kites above the street.
He lost his brown dog the day after his grey wife,
buried them both under an allotment compost heap.
In summer, we drank fizzy drinks burped a cow-choke,
spat onto the tarmac with brick coloured lips.
Our voices swapped words, like lego for beer, or ice cream
for a spliff. We went beyond the adult world, escaped
this earth, but soon found it again in the workplace.

Some Things That Have Happened So Far G Culshaw

I Was Once A Spy In Russia

Lived inside a grizzly bear and juggled balls outside
the Kremlin. Downed vodka through a hot-chip mouth.
Listened to Tchaikovsky inside the bear's skull.
Only once did we raise suspicion, when I was hungry
and walked into Mcdonalds. The FSB watched me pay
with my mobile. Followed me back to the forest
where I lived in a tree. I had four sim cards all snug
in the branches. A laptop dressed as a roof tile, two
handguns painted pink, and a microchip for my location
in the bear's left ear.
I watched the local news through shop windows,
kept an eye on limousines, painted pictures of armed guards
outside buildings of note. My boss told me to stay in
the shadows, and never growl. When winter came the bear
hibernated. We had an argument and he threw his contract
down the drain. A week later, they found it.
It popped up in the President's toilet bowl. The FSB chased
us through Moscow. The bear got arrested. He told them everything
after being teased with a feather duster. I became a waitress,
and a new spy for a local restauranter, whose brother-in-law
owned a cafe up the road. I sent him the menu inside a can
of coca cola. Found out the bear went to the circus for a job.

Some Things That Have Happened So Far G Culshaw

His Boots

I was in his boots again
carrying the weight
and wait;
I could smell his fingertips
on the boot laces
the dirt and grime
that he shovelled out
of the earth's skull
with his shoulders and hands.
Such iron tendons that held
my teenage years
nurtured them to grow
brought them up
from the ground below.

Some Things That Have Happened So Far G Culshaw

Gas Lamps

His wheels spun the light
down as he made his way around.
The roads held onto a glow
from the whittling away of gas.
He climbed frames of open
space for his feet.
The now angled bicycle
held time.
Each lamp refilled
to create the jigsaw
pieces of light
that lay on the pavements
and roads
after he'd left.

Some Things That Have Happened So Far G Culshaw

Taid

When the lid closed I stood
with eyes open, arms closed.
I sat on a hungry earth
that weaved around me
like a spider with prey.
I stood in his dark clothes
that lay on the floor,
watched them melt into the ground.
For years the earth didn't stop,
whisked my days into night.
I felt I was inside a pepper pot
looking up at the stars.
I hoped he would stretch an arm
through a seeded dandelion
cloud. But he never did.
I longed for the alleyway
and squeaky gate, tomatoes
on the window sill, opening
the coal shed door for tools.
Hear his voice break my mornings.

Some Things That Have Happened So Far G Culshaw

Yoke

I brought four carrier bags out of there
emptied the heaviness as a truck with sand.
Mainly football programmes of matches
mum went to see when her voice was strong,
and her knees stood as oaks in the wind.
Their house thins out, as I fill mine.
I yoke the weight of memories to the car.
One bag holds a wooden rattle that hides
the clacking boot studs in its handle.
Autographs scribbled, fingerprints rubbed
away. Folded tickets and scarfs last worn
when mum had the years ahead of her,
instead of behind as a ported ship with the tides.
I cross the road, carry years in my hands,
feel the weight of a childhood I once knew.
The bag handles stretch away from me,
strangle the sunlight out of my palms,
and I close the boot to hide what they have lost.

Some Things That Have Happened So Far G Culshaw

The Sea-front

The sandy air filled the train station.
We crossed a platform bridge
felt the world expand between our toes.
Ladybird-shaped taxis waited outside, luggage
cases blocked pavements, a salmon sky
topped off the buildings.
We walked down a crabbed road. The seas
breathe entered our lungs, our feet turned
into sand lizard quickness.
My gelled hair became holly tough
from the breeze.
Arcade machines talked to our wallets.
We entered the doughnut sea-front
saw waves crash into shin bones.
Heard a gull giggle, a pigeon gargle.
The world turned under our feet,
but we were not going anywhere.
We flicked on arcade lights and spoke
new words laughed at adults who wore
clothes we were yet to buy.
When we spent up we left the horizon
talked to the train wheels that brought us home.
At night, when I closed my eyes, I still smelt
the salt & vinegar, heard the grains of sugar
on my pillow. My feet flicked out sand
that pebbles had sneezed in the wind.

Some Things That Have Happened So Far G Culshaw

We Went Again Years Later

We went again years later.
I saw gaps in teeth like open gates.
Windows were chipboard colours.
Arcades begged for our coins,
and the crazy golf course peeled
away in the wind. The murky tea
stayed far out. Woodlice pavements
told us where the memories lay.
Music blasted from speakers,
shook the ice cream cones an old
man carried to his wife.
We walked past the bowling alley
heard the ten-pins yelp. We saw further
down the road today than years ago.
Each step made our head turn.
Footballs filled metal baskets
basketballs filled metal baskets.
Hats hung from shop entrances
lights flashed outside a market
sugar dummies plugged voices.
Cracks appeared in the council slabs,
signs of a parched landscape,
vacant of feet to keep it moist.

Some Things That Have Happened So Far G Culshaw

The Matchstick

She came into our lives like a lit
match. Burnt brightly, gave a glow
to the house. We had shadows
by her flame.
But then she ran down to nothing,
left us looking at a blackness
that has never given us any light.
So we carry on in the eclipse.

Some Things That Have Happened So Far G Culshaw

Fire Years

When mother lost her daughter
the house raged a fire
for ten years.
I sat there being burnt;
All I wanted was quietness.
But they carried on, threw
balls of fire over my head.
I never understood silence.
Until I left home years later.
Lying under a ceiling I hated
and opening a door
I didn't have the key for.

Some Things That Have Happened So Far G Culshaw

Going To Work Empty

The sunlight falls off the sky as a shade from a vase.
Sheep coordinate the night out of the fields, allowing hedgerows
to breathe in the growing light. A tractor wakes me up as I sludge
into the half-dark with hands in pockets. I have no idea
where they end. Fog pants out of me.
There's something of the known in this unknown, similar to passing
a hammer to a tradesman. The weight never leaves you even
when free of it. I shoulder my day's shift on the left side balance
out where I woke up this morning.
A bird catches itself flying across my eyeline. Puddles hold
themselves together in the dips of this road. Headlights furrow
into my skull before drifting by like I was the one moving faster.
I use my legs as a woodlouse walking across a stoney driveway.
There's a touch of this sky missing that I won't know until I reach
the end. My feet leave a part of me behind as I step
into the short future, walking away from a longer past.

Some Things That Have Happened So Far G Culshaw

The First Ten Years Of My Life

I lived between two people.
One was a blue, the other
a red. One had the glass
half full; the other
had the glass half empty.
One spoke, one didn't.
One pulled me this way
the other pulled me that way.
I felt I was in the middle
as I yoked their lives.
I had to walk along,
and let them clash.
Sometimes I would buffer it.
But other times when I wasn't
there, I came into carnage.
One tongue sat silent,
the other flickered like a lit
match. Though neither knew
the buckets of tears I
held across my shoulders.

Some Things That Have Happened So Far G Culshaw

I Read Them Now

I go there to read them these days.
When we use to stand at train
stations watch carriages
fly past like someone unfurling
a roll of ribbon. Mother sat
on a wooden bench, lost behind
her conker eyes. Father walked
to the end, then back again,
his mind whistling and hands
gloved by his pockets. There
were evening walks to the take-away
or chippie, grumblings when
we had to go shopping. The concrete
steps near Everland Chip shop,
where we would sit and the grease
tanned our fingertips, vinegar twitched
our nose. Those moments between
the arguing, which you never mention,
but I hold them like the rings in a tree.

Some Things That Have Happened So Far G Culshaw

The Tail End Of Belongings

I am going through the tail end
of what I left behind. From a dozen
years ago when life was leaner,
and I packed my bags to wander.
Here I am moving back and too,
sifting through a pile of things,
dates long gone, smeared dust,
money earned, wasted away.
Then I see the first football boots
I wore. They made my feet
tighten up, anchored my legs
until I learned how to use them.
A photo slipped from under a book,
my face from my early twenties.
Eyes alert like a tiger, skin well ironed,
the photo had promise. I opened
a wardrobe, then closed it,
as if it didn't exist. I thinned out
the house, watched more of my life
end up in a wheelie bin.
Listened to the world outside
like there was a seashell at my window.

Some Things That Have Happened So Far G Culshaw

A Letter To Tom

Stanley street still slips into the land
as if journeying to a secret hiding place.
Chimney pots peek out of the slates,
and cars squeeze between chit chat pavements.
I know your footsteps lie on the path, though
winds brush more of you away each year.
The disused gasworks now full of families
who live in brick igloos. Plastic rooftops
smile frost in morning, crack rain when it falls,
hold sunlight in orange peel evenings.
The police station, though empty,
keeps punching its thumb of glass and concrete
into the umbrella of a Wrexham sky.
A shopping complex called Eagles Meadow
shoulders a skyline you never saw.
Gone are the days of the Asda flyover,
and market stalls, when canopies roofed
people's mouths from summer rain.
The overgrown entry we use to cut through,
to leave roads to themselves, is tarmac smooth.
Gone the warped steps we hated to tread on
when leaves left slug wetness on the unknown.
Wind-trapped crisp packets, chip trays, empty cans,
scolded apple cores, orange peels, pigeon shit,
wiped away for pedestrians by a road sweeper.
Footsteps hold prints of people you've never heard.
Albert Street has become one-way and Bury Street,
still too tight to walk down, or shoulder slump drive.
There is a sign at the top of your street
'No contractor vehicles' and another
about the bumps in the road, but you
may know that one?
The cherry tree carries on growing,

Some Things That Have Happened So Far G Culshaw

as too, the oaks, that stand in front
of Derby Villas. Plumes of hope hide
the choked flats from spring to autumn.
Above your home clouds pass as spoken
library words. They bring back the sea
you knew as a young father and husband.
Stanley Villa house hides further away
from the greenery that swells behind
its walls. All this time and the front door
still eludes my eyes.
I haven't seen Mr Forbes and his wife
for years. Their daily walk on streets
I once knew now lost to the Obituaries.
Dot is struggling by the way. She has two sons,
and lives half-way up. I think her husband
left earth last year.
The old post office is a new one.
People don't sign on anymore
as the internet deals with all that stuff.
The queues you stood in lost
to the silence that comes through
the door each morning.
Kwik-save is Farmfoods.
Everything the same, but different
labels on shopping bags.
The white flats you hated have been
knocked down. The slabs of pebble-dashed
concrete gone from the eye, but not our
fingerprints. Houses bring gardens, doorbells,
kettle-people. The sky is much bigger
now over Hightown, allows more light.
Streetlights, perked up, rub away shadows
you stopped walking through at night.
The path along the old railway line
is still drawn. Paw-prints from your dog,
Lucky, tampered further since she left,
fossilised into this spinning earth.
The grass grows, but is hurdled with bramble,
nettles totter in the breeze, and birds

peck at the muted earth before the cars
slide down Derby Hill to unzip the morning.
The garden walls, built before
you moved, are standing firm against
the changes of voices and Climate Warming.
For some reason the streetlamps are the same.
For some reason the streetlamps are the same.
Your front door has a hanging basket.
Flowers crawl out of the wall and hang
over the metal bowl. There's a satellite dish
near the window brings a new world to your
living room. The privet hedge has grown since
you last clipped it. Big enough to goblet bird
nests and keep away wind that trips down
the gradient of the street.
Your backyard turned into a garden.
The walls knocked down that once hemmed
an alleyway. The brick floor you made suppresses
the dark. Moss bubbles in the damp areas.
The big wall still white from when we painted
it years ago with turps-cleaned brushes.
That first morning as the sun fell on it,
and we had to close our eyes from the bleach
brightness. The two shelf brackets beak
off the house. Some years you had hanging
baskets, but as you aged, they caught rust.
Mum is in a Nursing Home. Her legs lost
the will to stilt her body. Her eyes stay bright,
but her hair is pinched of youth. She is a shipwreck,
and listens to the television each day for a way out.
The voices form strings of noise in her head.
A magnified sun is outside, but curtains keep
it away. Mum hangs onto her smile,
as an autumn tree with fissured leaves.
Pills are given to her every three hours hide
the loss of her daughter that ferrets inside.
Arthritis ravaged her bones, stealing life's oil.
Her joints creak as pine trees in a storm.
The ceiling is the first and last thing she sees.

Some Things That Have Happened So Far G Culshaw

Father comes most days brings his accent
to her bedroom. Then he is gone, as a draft
that sneaked through an open window.
Wind brushes away my skin leaves me
feather-plucked raw. With mother in a home
my mind slopes back to the past. The family
days on the train, or Christmas dinner at our place.
The occasional visits back home that tapped
a mute button on her T.V remote.
I hope one day you see each other again.
I hope one day you see each other again.
I live in a village now. Town became too busy
for my ears. A girl brought something new
to my eyes. She allows me to be a poet.
The house I live in is made of stone. A material
you would nod as a membrane for a home.
We have a back garden that's separated
from a field by a fence. Jackdaws flick out
springtime when the light stays. A rookery
is on a corner of the road. They bring
their weekend rabble to every day of the week
in April and May. Tractors buff the road each hour,
shake the light off our roof. It's snow hushed here.
Trees bring wind and fields pop redwings, fieldfares
and skylarks. Dabs of sheep nip at the grass,
cows fill the land with ink blots.
The chiffchaff turns up around March. He sings
from a branch I do not know. Swallows arrive
a month later. They sit on the phone-wires
as a musical score. Some roads bend
while others go straight. But they all lead
to places you would know without seeing.
Time whittles my body my hair falls
away, grey shoots give me the look
of a decorator. My right shoulder keeps hold
of an old gym injury, and my knees get grumpier
with each dog walk or pull of sock. Sometimes
my hearing makes me think my ears have fallen.
I have two dogs, Jasper and Lana. They are collies.

Jasper has sandy fur and Lana is tri-colour.
She is stronger than him but he is quicker.
They both like to lick plates, or empty mugs
when we leave a room. They bark at neighbours,
postmen, Amazon guy, other dogs, cats, random noises
like slamming the dryer door, or dropping a book.
I look into Jaspers eyes and see you there
somewhere. We could have walked the three
dogs. Let them leave footprints in the wet mud.
Allow the sun to bake their prints hard until
the next grandparent and grandson come along,
and move our voices further down the lane.
I write poetry. I am a poet. Underneath my frown
and quietness, words simmered. One day they flowed
from my hand, I know you saw some rhymed poems.
Today I do free-verse. Life is simpler this way.
I read books, though I haven't started crosswords,
that you used to do in the local newspaper.
The questions in my head are too strong to not answer.
I hope one day I am puzzle free.
Your tools I was given ushered into a box outside.
Spanners, car light bulbs, wrenches, screw drivers,
socket-set, your fingerprints, whisper of oil,
and other metal things you needed for work,
but they're not for my hands.
Your binoculars allowed me to find out who I am.
When I first looked through the glass years ago
I saw myself in the distance walking away with my
life in the pockets. I had to chase him down and ask
for my time back. Now they lie under my bed like treasure.
Birds have come to my life, tree canopies, mountains,
cliffs and places I've never been. Remind me of you,
show me a world I don't see through my own eyes.
Remember those two holly trees in your back garden?
One grew berries the other refused. That year
when mistle thrushes turned up and picked the lot.
We sat in the dining room watching their beaks pinch
the fruit. Books came out, tea made, crumpets buttered,
scones sliced in half. We sat as fishermen on a pond's edge.

Some Things That Have Happened So Far G Culshaw

Neither of us spoke until they finished three days later.
We believed they were migrating and stopped
for a snack on their way home.
We agreed they were mistle thrushes.
We agreed they were mistle thrushes.
Today I sit in the living room, listen to the clock
work. Rustle a newspaper, wait for the kettle
to boil. I watch programs we watched,
try and repeat the days I have lost.
Those Sundays when you hated being
disturbed, answered the door with a nod,
sat on your tongue until the adverts.
I do this now. Sometimes the phone rings
and I sit waiting for it to rinse itself out.
The postman knocks on occasion,
the dogs bark, so I have to answer.
Christmas time the house is full. Too full.
That last Christmas I came to see you
after a two-mile walk. You'd moved into a flat.
People said you were safer there. I picked up
my legs and asked them to carry me to you.
I watched people take presents to houses
couples held hands as they walked pavements.
I heard songs and laughter, felt tomorrow's rain
on my skin.
The odd car went by crammed with smiles
and wrapping paper. Christmas trees
staggered on and off in the windows. A cat
sat on a gate-post. Children cycled
or skateboarded, let out their cracker jokes
as I trudged up the road. The sky on my back.
I had no idea if you were in or out. My eyes needed
to see you again ears wanted to hear the labour
of your clock as if an axe was chopping
the kindling of time to burn in the sun.
I cried all the way. All the way I cried.
All the way. My whole life poured out of me.
I dried my face before I knocked on your door.
Scrubbed the dirt off my skin that velcroed

onto me as I walked from my home.
You were full from dinner, and sat in your chair
like you had been dropped from the sky just for me.
The T.V spoke words, or it may have sung
hymns. You asked if I had eaten, I said 'Yes'
though I hadn't. I left home four months earlier
and for the next few years a hood
was put over the sunlight.
This was my first Christmas without mum,
and my last with you. If I had of known,
I would have visited you both.

Some Things That Have Happened So Far G Culshaw

The Follower

When I was young my father read the newspapers back to front.
He folded them in half, letting stories fall out onto the carpet.
He drank tea from a mug that suited his grip.
Buttered bread with his fingers holding the crusts.
I never saw him smile without reason.
He wore jeans, round neck jumpers, t-shirts
Clipped his nails in between sips of cold tea.
When he went to work I wore his slippers.
Combed my hair in his style. Picked up his mug.
Ran my hand down his corduroys.
I unfolded the newspaper and saw the pages were blank.
I knew then he had nothing to give me.

Some Things That Have Happened So Far G Culshaw

The day I left school I found an apple cut in half on the road.
Y diwrnod y gadewais yr ysgol darganfyddais afal wedi'i dorri yn ei hanner ar y ffordd.

Junior school plagued my childhood as a hornet stuck in my head.
Roedd yr ysgol iau yn bla ar fy mhlentyndod fel cacwn yn sownd yn fy mhen.

Some Things That Have Happened So Far G Culshaw

When I was a boy, I opened the curtains heard Beethoven
in the mouth of a blackbird.
*Pan oeddwn yn fachgen, agorais y llenni a chlywais Beethoven
yng ngheg aderyn du.*

I turned the corner like I was a tin opener.
Troais y gornel fel petawn i yn agorwr tun.

He watched from the side as the sun
does when lighting the moon
*Gwyliai o'r ochr fel mae'r haul
yn ei wneud wrth oleuo'r lleuad*

Some Things That Have Happened So Far G Culshaw

You tapped at things with your stick, prodded yesterday,
checked the edge of your eyebrows
Fe wnaethoch daro ar bethau gyda'ch ffon, prodio ddoe,
gwirio ymyl eich aeliau

Mother sat in the chair her body
a boulder I saw in Snowdonia.
Eisteddodd mam yn y gadair ei chorff
fel clogfaen gwelais yn Eryri.

The Nursing Home is a wood of fallen trees.
Mae'r Cartref Nyrsio yn goedwig o goed sydd wedi syrthio.

Some Things That Have Happened So Far G Culshaw

Acknowledgements

Butcher's Dog, Fenland Reed, The Birmingham Lit Journal, Reach, The Journal, Ginosko, Ink Sweat and Tears, Dreich, Rhodora, Smoke, and The Seventh Quarry.

Tresspassing – Winner of the RS Thomas Poetry Comp 2019
The Tale of Jarman Avenue – Long Listed in the Yaffle Competition.

Some Things That Have Happened So Far G Culshaw

www.ingramcontent.com/pod-product-compliance
Lightning Source LLC
Chambersburg PA
CBHW022041200426
43209CB00072B/1914/J